Pedal, Balance, Steer

Annie Londonderry, the First Woman to Cycle Around the World

VIVIAN KIRKFIELD

ILLUSTRATED BY ALISON JAY

CALKINS CREEK

AN IMPRINT OF ASTRA BOOKS FOR YOUNG READERS

New York

Annie wasn't afraid of hard work.
She bustled from room to room, cooking,
cleaning, and caring for her kids.
She hustled from business to business, selling
advertising space for local newspapers.
Times were tough. When Annie heard that
two rich businessmen were
going to pay ten thousand
dollars to the first woman
who pedaled around the world,
she knew she had to try. But
how on earth was a mother of
three, who had never even sat
on a bicycle, going to pedal
around the world?

The rules of the wager:
Bike around the world.
Speak only English.
Accept no donations.
Earn $5,000 while traveling.
Win $10,000 if you return in
15 months or less.

Annie remembered how hard it was to learn to speak English when she first came to America from Latvia as a little girl. And after her parents died, she took care of her younger brother and sister even though she was only a teenager. Now she had promised to do something no other woman had done before. But first things first: learn to ride. Annie signed up for lessons at a local bicycle academy. Neighbors scoffed. Strangers sneered. But Annie persevered.

On June 25, 1894, a crowd gathered at the Massachusetts State House in Boston. With only one extra pair of underwear stuffed in her pocket, Annie mounted her bicycle, waved farewell, and coasted down Beacon Hill.

PEDAL. BALANCE. STEEEEEERRR!

Outside the city limits, Annie's bike shook over uneven roads . . . when there were roads. She slogged through muddy tracks. She rattled over rocky trails. Her back ached, her corset pinched, her bottom begged to be anywhere but on a hard bike seat. Some days she only had an apple to eat. Some nights she slept on stony ground.

Ninety-two days later, Annie dragged into Chicago. Worn out from struggling with heavy skirts and an even heavier bike, she'd only covered one thousand miles—with twenty-four thousand still to go. It was already mid-September. The weather was turning colder. If she tried to cross the snow-covered Great Plains and Rocky Mountains on a bicycle, she would surely die. But Annie refused to give up.

Women all over the country read about her journey in their local newspapers and cheered for her to succeed. But not everyone cheered. Some accused Annie of being a bad wife and mother. Others didn't believe she was even a woman.

PEDAL BALANCE STEER

Ignoring the frowns, raised eyebrows, and pointing fingers,
Annie shucked off her skirts and put on bloomers. She checked
the map and charted her course. Instead of pedaling west to San Francisco,
she'd head back east and travel by steamship across the Atlantic Ocean
to France. Trading her forty-two-pound women's bike for a lightweight
men's racer, Annie set out for New York City. This bike was fast—but it
had no brakes. Pedal. Balance. Steer. Look oooouttt!

With a lighter bike and more suitable clothing, Annie made the trip to
New York City in record time—only eighteen days. She boarded a
ship bound for France, and quickly befriended fellow passengers. She
gave talks about her travels—and the audiences paid to listen to her speak.
That money would count toward the five thousand dollars she needed to earn.

But when the ship docked in Le Havre, her money was stolen. French officials confiscated her bicycle. She couldn't speak French. The officials didn't speak English!

Annie felt like someone had put the brakes on her plans.

With the help of an American diplomat, Annie persuaded officials to ship her bike to a representative of the Sterling Cycle Works in Paris. Annie hopped on a train and, as the landscape of France flashed by, memories of family flashed through her mind. Fifteen months was a long time to be away. But Annie was determined to win the wager, provide a better life for her children, and prove that a woman could take care of herself.

"Every few minutes I would shout 'Vive la France!' Then how they did cheer!"

Once in the city, Annie sold autographed photos, served as a clerk in different stores, and wheeled her way through the streets of Paris, adorning her body and her bike with ribbons advertising French companies, earning francs with every flutter.

As the wager clock ticked, Annie set out on the road from Paris to Marseille. On her bike she displayed the silk American flag she had received as a gift—it gave her a feeling of security.

But thirty miles outside of Marseille, catastrophe struck! Three men in masks jumped out from behind trees. Annie fell from her bike, wrenched her shoulder, and sprained her ankle.

The bandits searched her pockets. When the thieves discovered she had only three francs, they returned the coins, and Annie biked on, her swollen foot hanging over the handlebars.

Even with an injured foot, Annie was the darling of the people of Marseille.
She lectured at the Crystal Palace and gave exhibition rides.

Best of all, the camaraderie with fellow cyclists
warmed Annie's heart.

"My Stars and Stripes were hung from
a staff attached to my handlebar,
and it was heartily cheered."

After hearing about the
robbery, members of local
bicycle clubs refused to
allow her to ride anywhere on
French soil by herself, and wherever
Annie pedaled, they accompanied her.

But time was running short. Annie still needed to cross the continent of Asia, the Pacific Ocean, and the United States, from California to Chicago. Taking full advantage of the wager rules, she boarded a steamship bound for Alexandria, Egypt. From there she sailed to Singapore, Saigon, and Shanghai.

At each port, Annie rode her bicycle through the streets of the city, spinning stories faster than her bicycle wheels turned. Journalists printed her tall tales of hunting tigers in India, standing on the front lines of the war between China and Japan, and being rescued from a jail by forty French soldiers.

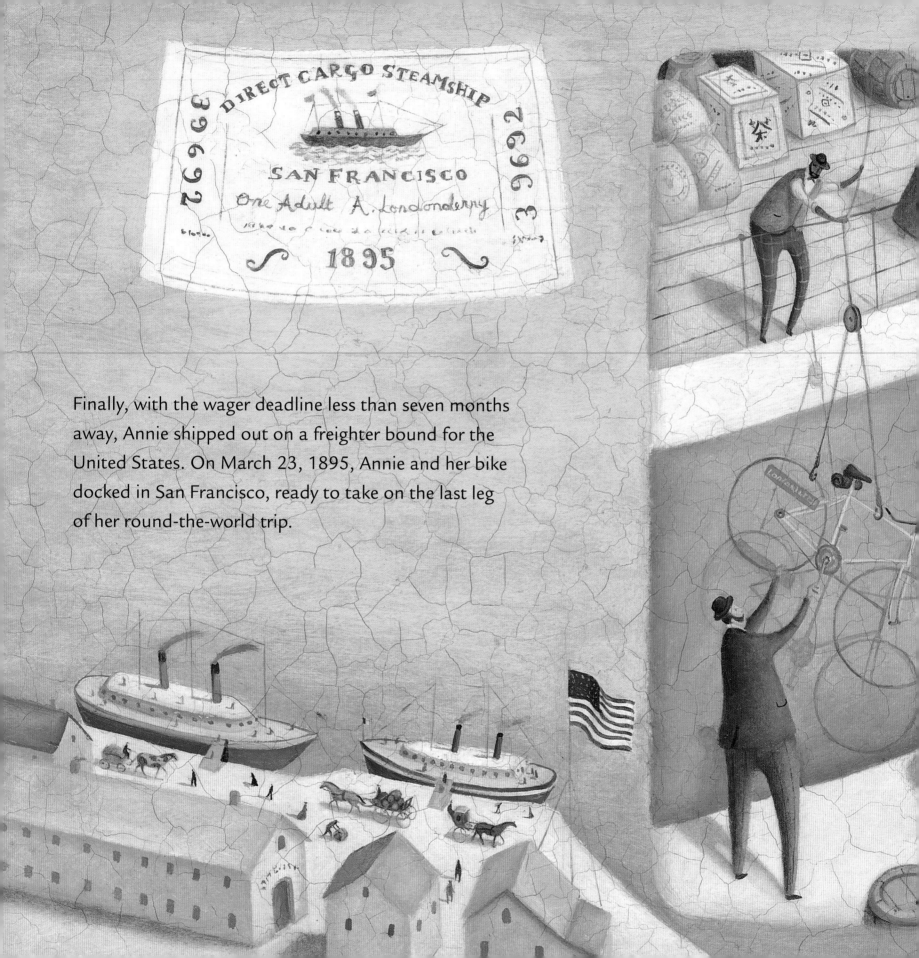

DIRECT CARGO STEAMSHIP

SAN FRANCISCO

One Adult   A. Londonderry

1895

396923 96923 9692

Finally, with the wager deadline less than seven months away, Annie shipped out on a freighter bound for the United States. On March 23, 1895, Annie and her bike docked in San Francisco, ready to take on the last leg of her round-the-world trip.

Earning money was still a concern. In a time when most men earned less than one thousand dollars a year, she needed to earn five! Still, Annie had never been afraid of working hard. In addition to selling her photo in every town along the route, she gave lectures about her travels.

Towne PORTRAIT STUDIO
425 Wash... St
BOSTON MASS

One afternoon, on her way to speak in Stockton, California, Annie raced
downhill on a narrow canyon road. A runaway horse and wagon
whizzed past. Annie smashed into a barbed wire fence.
Undaunted, she picked herself up, pedaled on,
and delivered her lecture the next night to
a sold-out crowd, despite a black eye,
scarred face, and a badly bruised body.

And it seemed the worst of her journey was ahead of her: one hundred and sixty-five miles of desert.

PEDAL! Each rotation of the wheel required more energy than Annie thought she could muster.

BALANCE! Her lips blistered, her legs buckled, and her eyes never wanted to see sand again.

STEER! She went without water.

But, women all over the world were counting on her to prove that a woman had the right to determine her own path in life. Annie had to finish.

She cut wood in exchange for a piece of stale bread. And finding a place to stay at night was challenging.

And finish she did! Fourteen days ahead of her deadline, to a cheering crowd, Annie cycled into Chicago.

She'd proven that women could ride bikes just as well as men.
She'd proven that *she* could do anything she put her mind to. Annie
Cohen Kopchovsky Londonderry had stepped up on her bike and
stepped out of the role society envisioned for her.
In her own words, she was a new woman.

PEDAL. BALANCE. STEER.

AUTHOR'S NOTE

Like Annie, I didn't have a bike when I was growing up. I lived on the Lower East Side of New York City, and my parents didn't have money for such things. But I watched other kids, and I knew it must be a wonderful feeling of freedom to ride one. I did get a bike of my own later in life, and when I discovered Annie's story, I appreciated the courage it must have taken to do something she had never done, go places she had never been, and leave behind everything she had ever known.

Her real name was Annie Cohen Kopchovsky. She took the last name of Londonderry for the duration of the trip— attaching a wooden sign with that name onto her bike— at the request of the Londonderry Lithia Spring Water Company of Nashua, New Hampshire, in exchange for one hundred dollars, making her one of the first women in sports to receive money for endorsements. This twenty-four-year-old Jewish mother of three was a most unlikely candidate for such a wager. But her idol was journalist Nellie Bly, who had traveled around the world eight years before to challenge Jules Verne's fictional record of traversing the globe in eighty days. Upon Annie's return, she moved her family to New York City, got a job as a journalist for the *New York World*, and published accounts of her exploits. Annie understood the power of personality and the value of a sensational story . . . and her tenacity knew no bounds. She was most definitely not afraid to work hard.

Annie Cohen Kopchovsky Londonderry, Chicago, September 1894. Annie sold autographed photos like this one throughout her journey to earn money.

BRAKES, BLOOMERS, AND OTHER BICYCLE BITS

The first bicycle was invented in 1817 by Karl Drais, a young man who wanted to travel faster than his own two feet could take him. Over the years, innovations like pedals, brakes, and better tires made the bike more popular. But it wasn't until 1885, when John Kemp Starley patented the Rover, the first commercially successful safety bicycle, that women flocked to ride it. With two wheels the same size, a chain drive, pneumatic tires, and more effective braking, it was safer, more comfortable, and more affordable than all those that had come before.

But riding a bike, even a safety bike, was not easy to do if you had to wear a tight corset that prevented you from taking a deep breath, a high collar that made it hard to turn your head, and a long heavy skirt that dragged on the ground and tangled in the bike chain. Soon women were experimenting with *bloomers*, so-called because Amelia Bloomer wrote about them in the newspaper she owned and edited. Some women slit their skirts and sewed seams to turn them into culottes. And others just donned men's trousers. Many people objected to women wearing pants. In fact, in many places it was against the law. But women who loved the freedom of riding a bike wore them anyway.

As Frances Willard, president of the Woman's Christian Temperance Union, had predicted, the bicycle "help[ed] women to a wider world." They were able to travel, get jobs, enter politics, have their voices heard. Elizabeth Cady Stanton, one of the leaders of the movement to gain voting rights for women, said that women were riding the bicycle to suffrage. And Susan B. Anthony, another strong voice for women's rights, said, "Let me tell you what I think of bicycling. I think it has done more to emancipate women than anything else in the world. It gives women a feeling of freedom and self-reliance. I stand and rejoice every time I see a woman ride by on a wheel." Even today, two hundred years after its invention, the bicycle still provides safe, affordable transportation, giving women more independence as they mount their steeds of steel and pedal their way to destinies of their own choosing.

Annie's 21-pound Sterling men's racer, San Francisco, spring 1895. The American flag gifted to her by an American diplomat in Paris is wrapped around the frame.

LANDMARK LAWS FOR WOMEN'S SUFFRAGE, BICYCLE MILESTONES, AND ANNIE'S JOURNEY

1777: The original thirteen states pass laws prohibiting women from voting.

1817: First bike invented by Karl Drais called the *Laufmaschine*, or *Draisine*.

1839: Mississippi grants women the right to own property (with their husband's permission).

1848: Declaration of Sentiments asks for an end to discrimination against women.

1858: Pedals added to bike.

1868: Pierre Michaux begins mass-producing bikes.

1869: First women's suffrage law in US passed in territory of Wyoming.

1869: William Van Anden receives a patent for the freewheel enabling the front wheel of a bicycle to spin without the rider pedaling.

1870: Annie Cohen is born in Riga, Latvia.

1875: Annie and her family immigrate to the United States and settle in Boston.

1886: Thomas Stevens becomes the first person to have cycled around the world.

1888: Inflatable bike tires are invented by John Dunlop.

1888: Annie marries Max Kopchovsky.

1890: Wyoming is first state to grant women the right to vote in all elections.

June 25, 1894: Annie accepts wager and leaves Boston to begin biking around the world.

September 24, 1894: Annie arrives in Chicago ready to give up, but changes her clothes and bike and continues on.

September 12, 1895: Annie completes her round-the-world circuit.

1920: First children's bikes are produced.

1920: Nineteenth Amendment ratified. The right to vote shall not be denied on the basis of sex.

1947: Annie dies due to a stroke.

1963: Equal Pay Act promises equitable wages for same work regardless of sex.

1964: Title VII of Civil Rights Act prohibits employment discrimination based on race, color, religion, sex, and national origin.

1972: Title IX prohibits sex discrimination in education programs that receive federal support.

1974: Equal Credit Opportunity Act outlaws lending discrimination based on sex or marital status.

1994: Improving America's School Act which provides funds to develop and implement model gender-equity programs.

An advertisement from the Londonderry Lithia Spring Water Company in the August 12, 1895, *Rocky Mountain News* of Denver announced Annie's visit to Colorado. The water company was Annie's first sponsor and paid her $100 to place the placard with the name Londonderry on her bike and use the name Annie Londonderry for the duration of her trip.

LONDONDERRY

MISS LONDONDERRY IN DENVER.

The Brave Little Woman Is In the Best of Health, and Says She Is Enjoying Her Tour Immensely.

COLORADO ROADS IDEAL FOR CYCLING.

Miss Londonderry left Boston last spring for a trip around the world on a wheel. It was a great and hazardous undertaking for a girl; but she possessed the courage, and will win her wager.

Miss Londonderry, before leaving this country, contracted with the

Londonderry Lithia Springs Water Company,

of Nashua, N. H., to use the name "Londonderry" on her journey, and to her great surprise the people of every country she visited were familiar with the name as being connected with the celebrated Londonderry Lithia Water. Thousands of people spoke of the excellency of this wonderful water.

Miss Londonderry has been highly entertained by wheelmen all through her journey. A large delegation of Denver cyclists escorted her into Denver from Colorado Springs. She will remain in the city a few days before taking up her journey eastward.

BIBLIOGRAPHY

All quotations used in the book can be found in the following sources marked with an asterisk (*).

Adams, Colleen. *Women's Suffrage: A Primary Source History of the Women's Rights Movement in America*. Primary Sources in American History. Mankato, MN: Rosen Central, 2003.

Blades, Nicole. "We Dare You: Break the Rules." *Bicycling*, December 16, 2015. bicycling.com/news/a20003949/we-dare-you-break-the-rules.

*Bly, Nellie. "Champion of Her Sex: Miss Susan B. Anthony Tells the Story of Her Remarkable Life to 'Nellie Bly.' " *World* (New York), February 2, 1896.

*Bly, Nellie, Junior. "Around the World on a Bicycle." *New York Sunday World*, October 20, 1895.

Bordin, Ruth. *Frances Willard: A Biography*. Chapel Hill: University of North Carolina Press, 1987.

Carson, Mary Kay, and Robert Hunt. *Why Couldn't Susan B. Anthony Vote?: And Other Questions About Women's Suffrage*. *Good Question!* New York: Sterling Children's Books, 2015.

Evelo. "Our Fave Five: Famous Women Cyclists You Should Know." The Evelo Blog. evelo.com/blog/our-fave-five-famous-women-cyclists-you-should-know.

Finison, Lorenz John. *Boston's Cycling Craze, 1880–1900: A Story of Race, Sport, and Society*. Amherst: University of Massachusetts Press, 2014.

Fotheringham, William. *Cyclopedia: It's All about the Bike*. Chicago: Chicago Review Press, 2015.

Gordon, Anna Adams. *The Beautiful Life of Frances E. Willard: A Memorial Volume*. Chicago: Woman's Temperance Publishing Association, 1898.

Guroff, Margaret. *The Mechanical Horse: How the Bicycle Reshaped American Life*. Austin: University of Texas Press, 2018.

Howat, Kenna. "Pedaling the Path to Freedom: American Women on Bicycles." National Women's History Museum, June 27, 2017. womenshistory.org/articles/pedaling-path-freedom.

Jensen, Linda. "Annie Londonderry." YouTube, September 14, 2017. youtube.com/watch?v=5Xgo4-HfUS4.

Kellet, Jim. "Women's Liberation and the Bicycle." YouTube, April 14, 2010. youtube.com/watch?v=_hD-dYL518vl.

LaFrance, Adrienne. "How the Bicycle Paved the Way for Women's Rights." *The Atlantic*, June 26, 2014. theatlantic.com/technology/archive/2014/06/the-technology-craze-of-the-1890s-that-forever-changed-womens-rights/373535.

L.A.W. Bulletin. "The Bicycle as a Reformer." *Courier* (Lincoln, Nebraska), July 17, 1895.

Lewis, Jone Johnson. "Who Was Frances Willard, Head for 2 Decades of the WCTU?" ThoughtCo, February 28, 2018. thoughtco.com/frances-willard-biography-3530550.

Macy, Sue. *Wheels of Change: How Women Rode the Bicycle to Freedom (with a Few Flat Tires Along the Way)*. Washington, DC: National Geographic Children's Books, 2017.

Maggs, Sam. *Wonder Women: 25 Innovators, Inventors, and Trailblazers Who Changed History*. Philadelphia: Quirk Books, 2016.

Mapes, Jeff. *Pedaling Revolution: How Cyclists Are Changing American Cities*. Corvallis: Oregon State University Press, 2009.

Marks, Patricia. *Bicycles, Bangs, and Bloomers: The New Woman in the Popular Press*. Lexington: University Press of Kentucky, 2015.

Mulder, Michelle. *Pedal It!: How Bicycles Are Changing the World*. Victoria, BC: Orca Book Publishers, 2016.

Murphy, Claire Rudolf. *Marching with Aunt Susan: Susan B. Anthony and the Fight for Women's Suffrage*. Atlanta: Peachtree Publishers, 2017.

Murphy, Liz. "Women's (Bike) History: Mary Sargent Hopkins." League of American Bicyclists, March 11, 2013. bikeleague.org/content/womens-bike-history-mary-sargent-hopkins.

"The New Woman Awheel." *San Francisco Call*, June 29, 1895.

Walljasper, Jay, and Melissa Balmer. "Ch 1 - Bicycling for Everyone." Pedal Love, July 20, 2018. pedallove.org/surprising-promise-of-bicycling-blog/2018/7/20/ch-2-bicycling-for-everyone.

Willard, Frances E. *A Wheel within a Wheel. How I Learned to Ride the Bicycle, with Some Reflections by the Way*. New York: F. H. Revell Co., 1895. archive.org/details/wheelwithinwheel00williala.

Zheutlin, Peter. *Around the World on Two Wheels: Annie Londonderry's Extraordinary Ride*. New York: Citadel, 2007.

———. "Women on Wheels: The Bicycle and the Women's Movement of the 1890s." annielondonderry.com/cycling-womens-rights.

ACKNOWLEDGMENT

With many thanks to Peter Zheutlin, great-grandnephew of Annie, and author of *Around the World on Two Wheels* and *SPIN*, a novel about Annie. One of the most important elements in crafting a nonfiction narrative is authenticity—I'm grateful for your feedback and support.

PICTURE CREDITS

Peter Zheutlin, annielondonderry.com: 34, 35, 37.

To my big sister, Rho: I'm grateful for your friendship and your love—
and for forgiving me even when I ruined your brand-new bike basket. —VK

For Mark, Never stop peddling, even though it might be time to buy
an e-Bike for those Derbyshire hills. Love from Alice x —AJ

Calkins Creek
An imprint of Astra Books for Young Readers, a division of Astra Publishing House
astrapublishinghouse.com

Printed in China

ISBN: 978-1-63592-682-8 (hc)
ISBN: 978-1-63592-683-5 (eBook)
Library of Congress Control Number: 2023904980

First edition

10 9 8 7 6 5 4 3 2 1

Design by Barbara Grzeslo
The text is set in ITC Legacy Sans Std.
The medium for the art was alkyd oil paint on paper with varnish.